PANZERKAMPFWAGEN

SKODA 35 (t)

Horst Scheibert

Schiffer Military/Aviation History
Atglen, PA

Photos:
Federal Archives, Koblenz
H. Scheibert Archives
Podzun-Verlag Archives
Heinrich Jürgens
Squadron/Signal Archives
H. Lücking

Front cover artwork by Steve Ferguson, Colorado Springs, CO.
Additional research by Russell Mueller.

THE FIELDS OF CASSEL

On May 29, 1940, a Skoda PzKpfw 35 (t) from the 6th Panzer Division fitted as a Befehlswagen (Pz.BefWg), slowly adavances in the twilight through a pasture near the village of Cassel, France.

Translated from the German by Dr. Edward Force.

Printed in the United States of America.
ISBN: 0-88740-678-5

This book was originally published under the title,
Panzerkampfwagen Skoda 35 (t),
by Podzun-Pallas Verlag.

We are interested in hearing from authors with book ideas on related topics.

Published by Schiffer Publishing Ltd.
77 Lower Valley Road
Atglen, PA 19310
Please write for a free catalog.
This book may be purchased from the publisher.
Please include $2.95 postage.
Try your bookstore first.

Skoda 35 (t) tank of the 7th Company, Panzer Regiment 11, in Paderborn, 1940.

Panzerkampfwagen 35 (t)

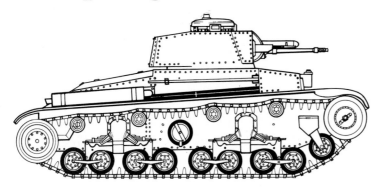

In 1935 the Skoda Works in Czechoslovakia introduced a new tank with a weight of eleven tons. The vehicle was designated Skoda LTM 35 and offered a number of progressive design features, which were later taken up by many manufacturers of armored vehicles. One of these features was the installation of the drive wheel at the rear of the vehicle instead of the front. This was decided in order to keep the fighting compartment free of the driveshaft and other moving parts. The drive train thus ran directly from the motor via the transmission and side shafts to the drive wheels. Pressure brakes, gears and steering were operated by compressed air. These were innovations that did much to ease the physical demands on the driver. An additional feature was the system of wheel suspension, which distributed the weight evenly among the small road wheels. This increased the life span of the tracks to an average of 6500 kilometers, while other tanks of the time attained a life span of only 1600 km for their tracks.

The primary armament of the LTM 35 was a 3.7 cm Skoda A-3 tank gun, which offered not only a good rate of fire, but also a high initial velocity with good ballistic characteristics, especially for armor-piercing shells. In addition, it had two machine guns, one installed in the turret, the other in the nose.

The vehicle was propelled by a straight six-cylinder Skoda T-1 engine, which produced 120 HP at 1800 rpm. The power-to-weight ratio was only 10.3 HP per ton, but a 12-speed gearbox with six forward and six reverse gears gave it good mobility. Its top speed was 34 kph, and

the fuel capacity was 186 liters, giving the vehicle a range of 190 kilometers.

The crew consisted of four: driver, bow gunner (radioman), loader and tank commander, who also had to operate the tank gun and thus served as the gunner. When Germany occupied Czechoslovakia in March of 1939, it took over the equipment of that country's armed forces. In particular, the Czech tanks were immediately introduced into the Wehrmacht. The LTN 35 was renamed Panzerkampfwagen 35 (t), and entire units (Panzer Regiment 11 and the independent Panzer Unit 65) were equipped with them.

This Czech-designed tank took part in the Polish campaign with those units. Because of its robust construction, it suffered very few losses on account of technical damage. During this campaign, though, one major disadvantage came to light, this being the construction of the chassis, hull and turret. Despite all its advanced design features, the Panzerkampfwagen 35 (t) was assembled with rivets, a technique that was obsolete in comparison with the welding technology of the Germans.

The PzKpfw 35 (t) also took part in the French campaign of 1940, where these tanks gave good service to the German Army. One reason being that another entire Panzer division (the 6th) was equipped with the 35 (t), and for another, the units equipped with them had greater firepower (the 3.7 cm tank gun), than other divisions which still used many Panzer Is and IIs.

When the Wehrmacht marched into the Soviet Union in 1941, there were still a number of PzKpfw 35 (t)s available for use by the Germans (now only the 6th PD), as well as the Hungarians, Rumanians and Italians. Again the rugged construction of these vehicles made it possible for them to play a significant role. During the winter of 1941-42, the coldest winter for twenty years in the Soviet Union, the German armies on the eastern front came to a standstill. Supply difficulties (what with the vast distances), partisan activity and extremely low temperatures created many problems for the Wehrmacht. The Panzer 35 (t) suffered more than other German tanks on account of their compressed-air system, which often froze. In this winter (1941-42), the last Skoda 35 (t) tanks – insofar as they were still on hand and usable – were withdrawn, and the 6th Panzer Division was transferred to France in the spring of 1942, where it was supplied with German-made tanks (Panzer III and IV) during the course of the summer.

This picture shows the original Czech camouflage paint. It consisted of three colors, with green and brown spots on a lighter background. In the German Army, all tanks were painted gray, the uniform color as of 1939.

This tank was developed by the renowned Skoda Works in Pilsen, Czechoslovakia, and stood out in terms of its modern design. After the occupation of Czechoslovakia in 1939, the German Wehrmacht took over about 300 tanks from Czech supplies.

A view from the turret hatch at the 3.7 cm tank gun, the 7.92 mm machine gun and the antenna on the left track cover.

Panzer Regiment 11 (Paderborn) of Panzer Brigade 6 and Panzer Unit 65 (Sennelager) of the 1st Light Division (Iserlohn) were equipped with these tanks. Panzer Regiment 11 was also subordinated to the 1st Light Division for the 1939 Polish campaign.

Left: Marching to the loading point; above and upper right: unloading; right: a marching company (1st Co., Panzer Unit 65), in the personnel car is the company chief, then come his two motorcycle messengers, followed by 22 Skoda 35 (t) tanks, consisting of the chief's tank, company-troop tank and four platoons of five tanks each. There was not much time for practice, for the units that were equipped with the new tanks had to take part in the Polish campaign just half a year later.

Shortly before the campaign, all German tanks had large white crosses painted on all four sides of their turrets as identifying marks.

Left: Two Skodas of Panzer Regiment 11, followed by a Panzer II, another Skoda and another Panzer II. Above is the tank of Hauptmann Mecke, Chief of the 2nd Co., Panzer Regiment 11, recognizable by number 200.

Upper right: fording the Warthe shortly after crossing the border (September 1939).

Right: Skoda 35 (t) of the staff of the 1st Unit (recognizable by the Roman I on the number plate) of Panzer Regiment 11.

The tanks soon proved to be very solidly built, with resulting sturdiness and long life. Because of their 3.7 cm guns, the 1st Light Division, which, unlike the other five Panzer divisions that existed then, no longer had any Panzer I tanks (armed only with machine guns), and thus became one of the strongest Panzer divisions of the time – as strange as it seems.

Both pages show Panzer Regiment 11 in action during the Polish campaign. Lower right: marching past the standard of the 1st Unit (pink-black-pink).

This page also shows pictures from the Polish campaign. The gun proved to be a very good weapon, which could fire explosive and armor-piercing shells.

Officers wore the black Schiffchen cap inside or outside the tank.

Photos from the 1939 Polish campaign. The roads in that country were poor and dusty. In addition, combat often required action in open country. Dusty faces (the dust came through all openings) and gritty teeth were always a part of this sunny autumn. Getting stuck in holes or swampy spots also happened often enough (above).

The losses in this campaign were not high. Above we see the shot-down, burned-out tank of the Chief of the 1st Co., Panzer Unit 65 (Hauptmann von Kriegsheim), and at left is the tank of Leutnant Wendt, which was hit by artillery fire.

Upper left: Polish soldiers surrender during the fighting between Modlin and Warsaw.

Graves of fallen Panzer soldiers.

These units gathered at specified assembly points when the campaign ended.

The tanks waited in parking areas to be transported homeward. The weapons (here machine guns) are already removed. This interesting picture shows a Skoda 35 (t) and a small armored command car I B, both of the 1st Unit of Panzer Regiment 11.

The winter of 1939-40 was devoted to intensive training. The experience gained in the first campaign had to be passed on to the troops. The slightly opened lid of the turret hatch was typical of this tank, as it afforded the commander a good field of vision. Only when the air contained a lot of shrapnel was it closed, and the battlefield was observed via optics and a hand periscope (for which there was an opening in the turret lid).

Training took place at the Senne training camp (where these two pictures were taken). Above: A tank of the 3rd Co., Panzer Regiment 11 (5th tank, 3rd Platoon). Right: near the German cross, the symbol of the 6th Panzer Division (previously the 1st Light Division) can be seen. This typical, unobtrusive cross (a stylized Iron Cross) was used as of 1940 in place of the wide, noticeable white cross.

The Campaign in France

In this campaign, the Skoda 35 (t), used only by the 6th Panzer Division, saw action in the advance to the Channel coast. Right: meeting with mountain Jägers in the Ardennes. Below: supporting the mass crossing near Montherme by firing on bunkers on the opposite shore. Lower right: Combat in Brunehamel.

Combat in Brunehamel. Here French
troops were surprised in their quarters,
and artillery marching through the
town was captured.

On the broad advance to the Channel. At left, the Chief of the 1st Co., Panzer Unit 65, Oberleutnant Dr. Bäke (Commander of the 13th Panzer Division in 1945!), receives from Battle Group Leader Oberst von Esebeck the order to advance on Hauteville on the Oise.

Below: destroyed Skoda 35 (t) tanks. The French tanks were not very mobile but heavily armed and armored.

Standing ready shortly before the attack. The chief's last communication with his platoon leaders. The swastika flags on the rear identified the tanks to their own aircraft.

A 35 (t) destroyed by British antitank guns and burned out during the street fighting at Cassel, near Dunkirk, Flanders.

Symbol of the 6th Panzer Division in the French campaign.

Symbol of the 6th Panzer Division as of 1941.

Attack of Panzer Unit 65 after breaking through the Weygand Line south of Rethel in the direction of St. Etienne. Skoda 35 (t), Panzer II and IV tanks can be identified.

The second meeting with the infantry.

The reserve company follows in line. The opening for the hand periscope can be seen in the hatch cover at left.

Before and in Epinal on the Mosel there was hard fighting once more at the end of the French campaign. Here a destroyed Skoda 35 (t) of the 1st Co., Panzer Unit 65, stands on a Mosel bridge in the city.

After their return to their new garrison in Bielefeld, the tanks march past the unit commander during the victory parade. Here we see the platoon leader (Leutnant Scheibert) of the 1st Platoon of the 1st Co., Panzer Unit 65.

At the barracks after the victory parade. Oberleutnant Dr. Bäke (Chief, 1st Co., Panzer Unit 65) wears the Schiffchen.

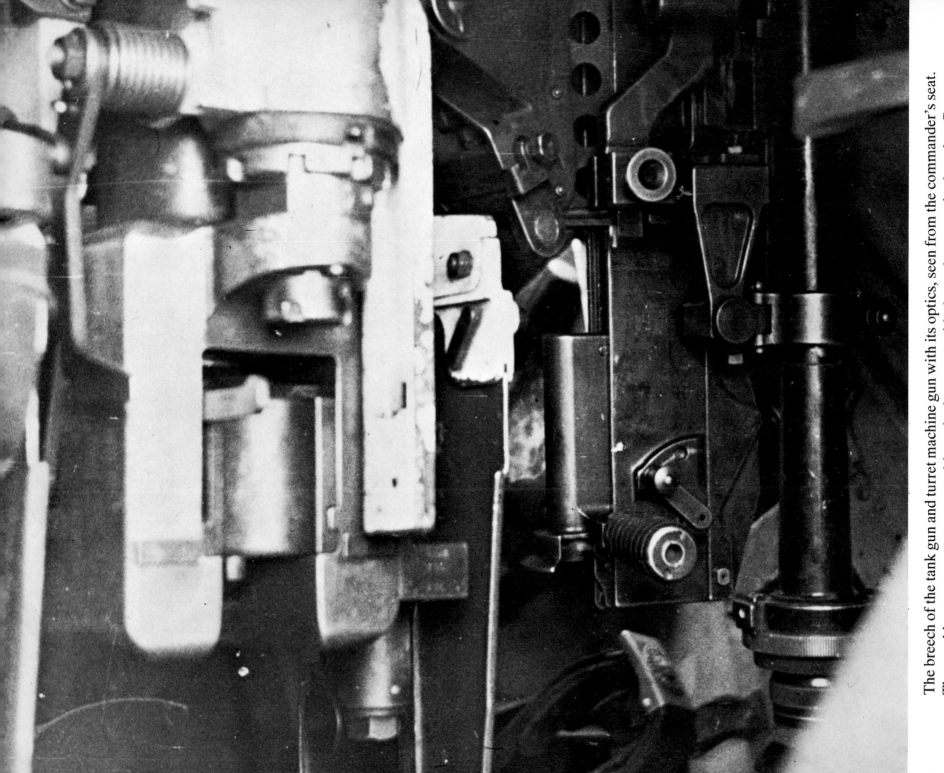

The breech of the tank gun and turret machine gun with its optics, seen from the commander's seat. The machine gun was not mounted in a single mount with the tank gun, as in the other German tanks.

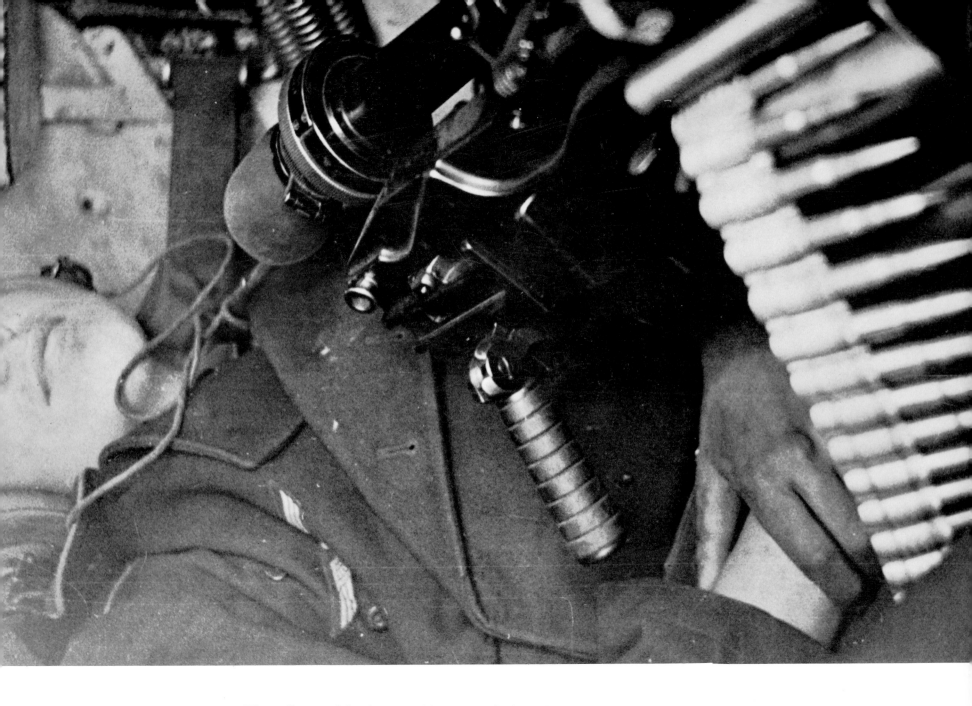

The radioman (also bow machine-gunner) sleeps behind his machine gun.

The driver – an Obergefreiter – sleeps at the controls after a long march. Behind him hang the cartridge belts of the turret machine gun and the headphones. Neckerchiefs were worn on account of the dust.

Unteroffizier Sprenger, Tank Commander of the 1st Co., Panzer Unit 65, enters the turret of his Skoda 35 (t). The rivets are easy to see, as is the leather padding on the turret hatch cover. Many a bullet or splinter got stuck in it if the cover could not be closed at the right time. The rivets proved to be inadequate when a heavy shell hit the armor plates at an angle and made them break loose.

The platoon leader's tank, 1st Platoon, 1st Company, Panzer Unit 65, at the training camp in Thorn on the Vistula during drills in the spring of 1941, before Operation Barbarossa (the Russian campaign) began.

A tank of the 1st Co., Panzer Regiment 11, with an interesting barrel brace above the track cover. It could hold additional fuel canisters, personal belongings of the crew, and the "food box" –usually an empty ammunition case in which food was carried.

Thorn, 1941: Two officers stand before a Skoda 35 (t) tank.
The officer at right wears the white peaked field cap (always
without a silver cord) and a rubberized motorcycle coat.

The tank was easy to steer thanks to its pneumatic servo steering, and did not demand as much physical strength of the
driver as the tanks made in Germany. The whistling of the air
jets gave it a characteristic sound. Its top speed was 34 kph.

Marching into the woods of the Memel area to attack the Russian troops in the Baltic area, June 1941.

This 10.5-ton Skoda 35 (t) served with the 1st Unit of Rifle Regiment 4 (note the standard). Its very rugged chassis allowed the tracks to last up to 6000 kilometers.

Tanks of the 1st Platoon, 1st Company, Panzer Unit 65, during the first days of the Russian campaign in the Baltic area. The crew sitting outside the tank, and the muzzle protector on the barrel, indicate a quiet situation. The pieces of tread on the front were to provide additional protection, the corduroy road on the track cover helped on soft ground, and the fuel canisters on the engine cover provided a greater range.

Encountering a Russian KW 1, three times as heavy, shot down by anti-aircraft fire before Pleskau. The Skoda's 3.7 cm shells could not threaten it.

On the bad roads in the direction of Leningrad, Skoda tanks also served to help wheeled vehicles that got stuck. On the cycle in the foreground, under the symbol of the 6th Panzer Division, the tactical symbol of the 9th Company of Rifle Regiment 4 can be seen. The (yellow) IT on the sidecar indicates that this BMW sidecar cycle belongs to the repair troop of this company.

The A 01 means: A = unit staff of an independent unit (here Panzer Unit 65) and 01 = the first tank, that of the commander, Oberstleutnant Schenk, who is in the turret. At left is Oberleutnant Marquart, the unit's adjutant.

Grenadiers who got a ride jump off the tanks; in the foreground is a Skoda 35 (t), behind it a Panzer IV.

Note the large containers on the track covers, the numerous fuel canisters on the engine cover, the steel helmets hanging on them, and the large bundle of luggage on this tank.

Tanks and grenadiers outside Leningrad. There was still hard fighting on the various defense lines outside this city in September 1941.

A Skoda 35 (t) tank and an SPW of the Panzer Grenadiers have fallen victim to a tank trap near Leningrad in 1941.

These action photos show the Skoda tank from all sides.

This is how it began. Designed in 1934, built in 1935. The weapons were made in the weapon factories in Brno, the rest was built and assembled at the Skoda Works in Pilsen. Its Czech designation was LTM-35 (S II a). In the picture at left, it still bears Czech army paint.

And this was its end, as mortar towing tractor 35 (t) in 1942-43. The general towing tractor 35 (t) looked similar.

Panzerkampfwagen 35 (t)

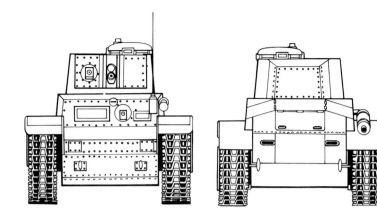

Technical Data
Panzerkampfwagen 35 (t)

Manufacturer	Skoda
Years built	1935-1937
Number built	over 300
Crew	4 men
Weight	10.5 tons
Length	4.47 meters
Width	2.13 meters
Height	2.19 meters
Motor	Skoda T 11 6-cyl. (water-cooled)
Power	120 hP at 1800 rpm
Gears	6 forward, 6 reverse
Track width	320 mm
Ground clearance	350 mm
Armor plate	Front 25, sides 16, rear 12 mm
Armament	1 Skoda 37 mm L/40, 2 MG Type 37
Ammunition	90 37-mm shells, 2550 7.92-mm rounds
Fuel capacity	153 liters
Fuel consumption	Road 80 l./100 km, off-road 120 l./100 km
Range	Road 190, off-road 120 km
Top speed	34 kph

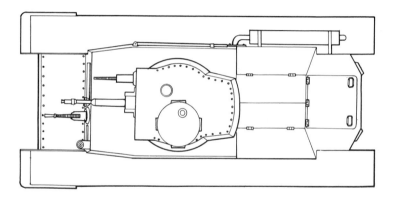

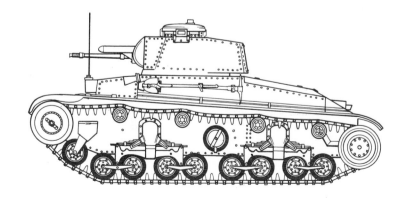

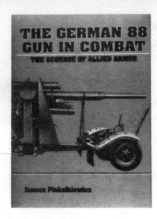

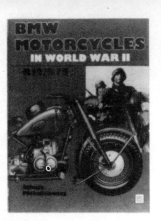